Carving Found Wood

Written by Vic Hood
Photography by Jack A. Williams

FOX CHAPEL
PUBLISHING

ISBN: 978-1-56523-159-7
Library of Congress Control Number: 2002102596

To learn more about the other great books from Fox Chapel Publishing, or to find a retailer near you, call toll-free 800-457-9112 or visit us at *www.FoxChapelPublishing.com*.

We are always looking for talented authors. To submit an idea, please send a brief inquiry to acquisitions@foxchapelpublishing.com.

Printed in the United States of America

Acknowledgments

The authors would like to extend appreciation to all of the carvers who allowed us to showcase their work in this book. Without their kind patience and talent, this book would not have been possible. We would also like to express our gratitude to Leigh Ann Hood for her diligent work in transcribing the interviews and to Angel Loupe for her assistance in document transcription. We would also like to recognize the significant contributions of Sharon McPherson, who helped to format the dialogue into a more consistent presentation, and Lillian Perkins, for her proofreading skills and editorial input. A very special thanks is extended to Carole Williams for her hundreds of hours spent in photographic editing and to Don Dubenbostel for the photographs of the authors.

Table of Contents

Driftwood

Bristle Cone Pine

Artists

Cypress Knees

Slab

Introduction

This book is intended as a photographic essay about found wood carving and the potential of the medium to create art. The term "found wood" applies to wood that is carved in its natural or unaltered condition. The most commonly thought of found wood is driftwood; however, there are several kinds of found wood that are being used today to create art. Other examples include dead falls, the most popular of which is bristle cone pine and western juniper; bark, the most widely used is cottonwood bark because of its thickness and ability to hold detail; cypress knees, desired for the unique shapes and natural lines; and slabwood, the discarded portion of a tree when it is sawn into lumber.

The gallery portion of this book illustrates the wide variety of uses of found wood in carving. The pieces shown here are carved by award-winning carvers from all over the United States. Each of these carvers will give you an insight into his or her art, inspirations, and technical aspects of dealing with found wood. You will find helpful information about acquiring found wood, carving and finishing techniques.

The step-by-step project is carved in cottonwood bark. Wherever possible when a feature was developed on one side the corresponding side was completed to give you a visual of the completed form and the ongoing process of the symmetrical side.

We attempted to diversify the subject matter to illustrate the wide range of creative application in found wood. In this book we have presented the human face and form, realistic animals, interpretative birds and animals, mythical styled houses and caricatures. We hope as you read this book that you are inspired by some of the wonderful carvings to create your own masterpiece in found wood.

—Vic Hood and Jack A. Williams

Marshal Artime

Marshal Artime, a father of six children and grandfather to 12, lives in Addieville, Illinois. He first started carving in 1974 but didn't get truly serious about the artform until he retired from a job as an auto parts sales executive in 1985. Like a good many other carvers working now, he was inspired by John Burke, an award-winning carver who conducts numerous demonstrations at shows in the Midwest. Marshal is a member of the Belleville Area Holzschnitzers Carving Club. He specializes in carving large busts of western, rural figures and cottonwood bark. Artime's favorite found wood medium is bark.

Style and Character in Bark

Marshal Artime

What I enjoy about bark is that each piece has its own individual style and character. You really have to go with the flow. It's not like having a log where you can measure and plan in advance. With bark you have to get into it first to see where the good and the bad areas are and see what the bark might look like—an old man, or a sea captain, or an Indian or whatever else you find to do. Working through the bad areas keeps it interesting.

I get my bark from a lot of different places. There's a lot of difference in bark depending on where it came from. The bark from the mid-west is very dense—the layers are close together. A lot of bark in our local area has so much air in it that you can't carve into it; it has no density at all.

One thing I like about bark is that I can carve it easily and fast. But the most important thing to me is the rustic effect I can get by carving around the natural features that are unique to each piece. Even if I didn't carve it, the bark would have a completely individual and interesting effect. A 12" x 12" x 6" piece of butternut or some other straight wood would be the same all over—monotonous.

I carve a lot deeper on bark pieces than might seem sensible, sometimes leaving only a quarter inch. That way I get strong profiles in faces and create more shadows in the features.

Bark has its problems. It chips and pieces break off. Sometimes I need to glue bits back on. For example, in working around eyes I have to be really careful to make small movements. When I'm cutting the pupil, which goes all the way to the back, I push a small gouge in as deep as I can, because I know that even if some wood breaks off I'll still be able to see the

pupil. The wood here is so soft that to open the iris up I just have to move the gouge from right to left.

For finishing I use oil paint, thinned down so it is more like a stain. I let it dry for 24 hours and then spray on about six light coats of a Krylon matte spray without buffing between coats. That way I can control the sheen and end up with a satin luster instead of a high shine. For the top finish I use Watco Finishing Wax mixed half light and half dark. Bark is so dark itself that you can't use the wax 100% dark. After that I give it a final buffing.

All the accessories are carved out of bark. For an effect of real ash in the pipes I just dab on a little white oil paint and blend it in. That quality to blend easily is why I prefer oil paints; acrylics dry too fast.

I make some pieces to hang and some to stand alone. For the standing ones I cut a slice off the carving's back and use that for a base. On the hanging pieces I carve a hole in the back so that it can be hung on a drywall screw or a nail. This is a lot better than putting attachments on the back that might come loose and damage the wood. I make sure it will hang plumb by putting most of the bark on the bandsaw before carving to give it a flat back. Then I hold the finished piece with two fingers in the hanging-hole to see if it veers off-plumb.

In an average year I make approximately 100 bark carvings. Some of them are small, like the Santas, which I can make pretty fast. But about 35 are larger, serious pieces.

I like wood carving better than any other form of art because you basically start with a piece of nothing much—just a piece of wood—and make it come to life, seeing the actual personality come out of the wood. That's something drawing or painting on a flat surface can't do. The hard part is coming up with the ideas, but sometimes I get help from the bark itself when it pushes you in one direction or another and suggests its own form. There's a lot of satisfaction in that.

Marshal Artime

Marshal Artime

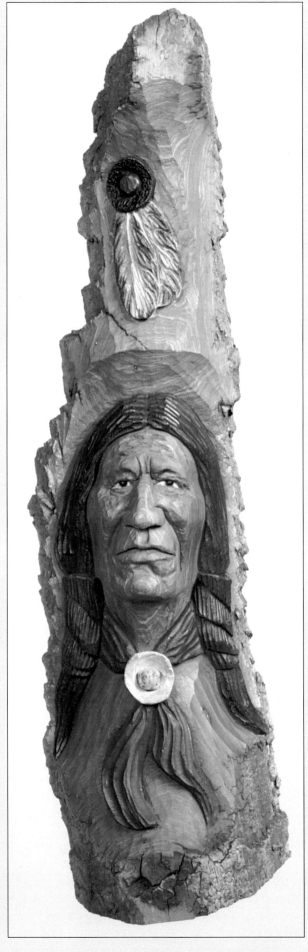

Marshal Artime

Marshal Artime

Carving Found Wood

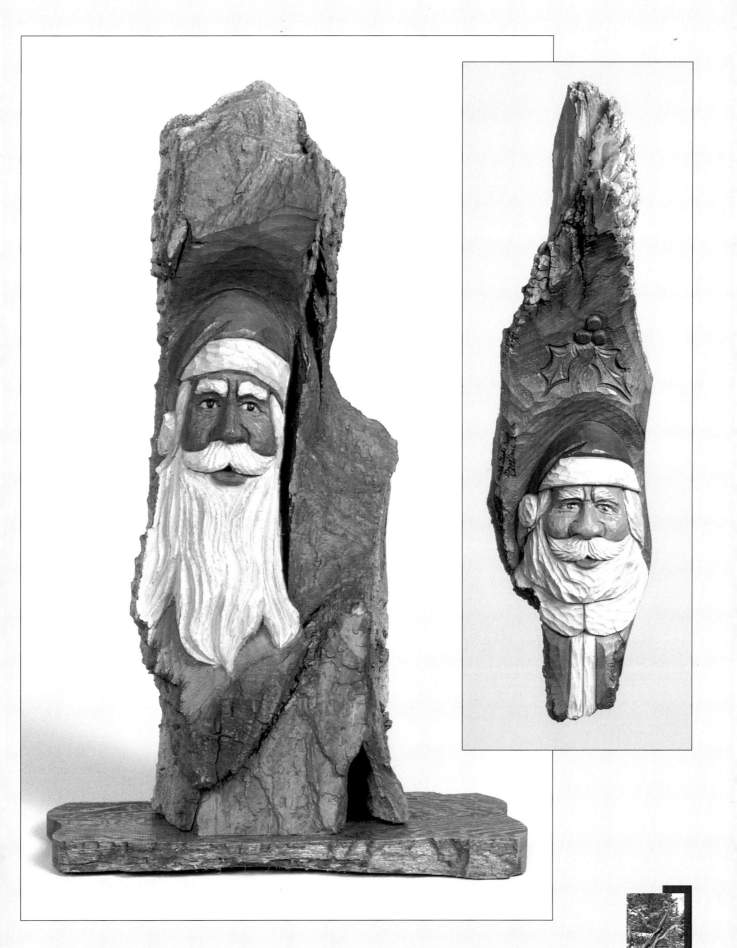

Marshal Artime

Carole Jean Boyd

Carole Jean Boyd's unusual choice of found wood is cypress knee, on which she carves human faces and figures. She is a noted teacher of carving who spends weeks on the road every year and less and less time at her home in Alabama.

Before becoming a professional woodcarver, Carole Jean was a photographic artist for 27 years. Her primary work was in negative retouch and painting of finished photographs. This is how she became familiar with faces and developed her sense of design. Painting the photographs also influenced her techniques in finishing her woodcarvings.

Although she has completed a wide range of projects, Carole Jean specializes in the "gift-giver type" of carvings such as Father Christmas and Santas.

Carole Jean started carving in 1987 and has been teaching for 11 years in venues all over the United States. She has taught at numerous schools, such as J. C. Campbell Folk School in Brasstown, North Carolina; The Southeastern Woodcarving School in Mercedes, Texas; War Eagle; and others. She has taught in carving clubs all over the United States. She is an award-winning carver whose accolades include Best of Show at the Blue Earth Show in Minnesota. Carole Jean won first place in numerous competition shows, including the International Affiliated Woodcarvers Congress, Dollywood Woodcarving Showcase, Wonders in Wood, the Mid South Show, the Southeastern Woodcarvers Competition and others.

Carole Jean has written several articles for *Chip Chats* and *Wood Carving Illustrated* magazines.

IN THE COLLECTION OF DR. & MRS. MARK KINDRICK

Cypress Knee Figures & Spirits

Carole Jean Boyd

I came to woodcarving by an irregular route, so you couldn't say it's the fulfillment of a childhood dream. My original career was as a photographic artist. As it turned out, 27 years of studying the human face was helpful for my carving. For a good many years my husband and I did soft sculpture and sold our work at craft fairs. After his death I just didn't have the motivation to continue something we had always done together, so I made one last trip to a craft fair to dispose of the inventory.

By some kind of good fortune I set up next to a wood carver who studied my sculpture and said, "Now if you can do that, then you can carve." He and his wife kept after me until I went to a carvers' meeting with them. They put me down next to a man who was carving a spirit face out of a little split log, gave me a knife and a piece of log, and told me just to do everything he did. I've been carving ever since.

Carving cypress knees was kind of an accident, too. Early on I was carving because I wanted to do dolls, and the man who started me carving told me it would be best to start with a clothed figure. My brother had a cypress knee that looked to me like a woman in a long gown or coat. So that's what I made. Santas also seem like natural shapes for cypress knees, and I've done a world of them.

I get my material already stripped and cleaned. Cypress knees are not the sort of thing you're going to go out and pick up yourself. Cypress knees are very soft. That makes them easy to carve in some ways, but it also causes problems. Sometimes the wood mashes down instead of slicing the way harder woods do; and the only cure for that is keeping the tools very sharp.

I don't have a single word to describe my work. It isn't realistic; it isn't caricature; it isn't primitive. Maybe it's a blend of all three. I do put an unusual amount of detail into my work, so perhaps that is its distinctive mark. Most of this I achieve with burning tools, especially the feather burner. I got the idea from the bird carvers, and thought, "If they can do that with feathers, I can do that with hair."

My two best sellers are Father Christmas and spirit faces. On the former I do quite a lot of painting but not in the traditional bright red. I use oil paints in subdued burgundies, light blues, and mustards—soft colors like you see on nineteenth-century postcards. The spirit faces I paint very little, maybe just brush the cheeks and paint the eyes. The natural color of the wood is much closer to skin tones than any paints.

I have experimented with a variety of finishes. Lately I have been using motor oil with mineral spirits. I read about this strictly non-traditional approach in a carving magazine and knew that I had found a substitute for the boiled linseed oil I hate because it smells so bad. Motor oil works just fine; but if you use it everywhere on the surface the wood all turns out the same color.

Cautiously used, motor oil exposes the grain, and cypress knees have an exceptionally interesting grain of which most people aren't aware. On top of the oil, or oil and paint, goes Deft. I use it on everything I carve. Then I may use steel wool, vacuum the piece thoroughly, and give it another coat of sealer.

Since I started on them in 1990, I would say I have carved over a thousand cypress knees, and there's still something to learn from each one. That's an important thing about woodcarving; you keep on learning. Even though I'm a teacher now, I still take classes from others, like the bear carving class I took recently. Animals are not really my thing; I do faces and human figures. But even if you take away only one thing you didn't know before, every class is worth the effort.

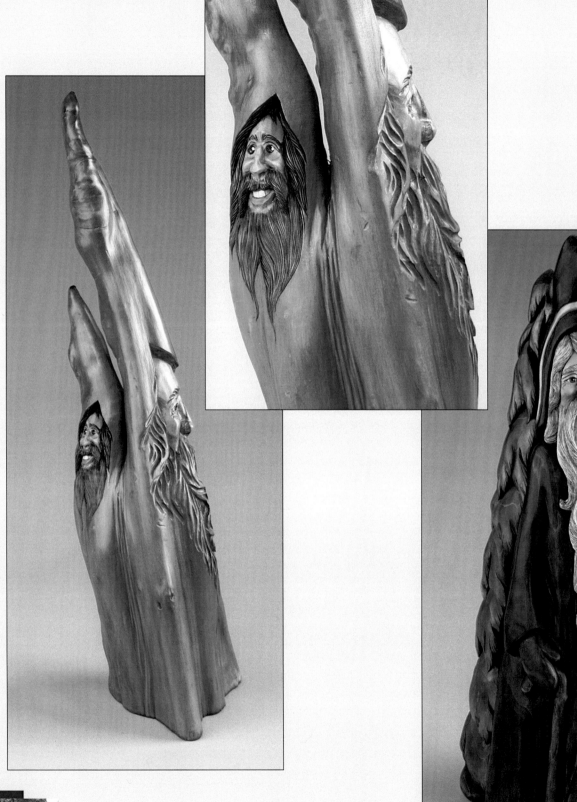

Carole Jean Boyd

Carving Found Wood

Carole Jean Boyd

Carole Jean Boyd

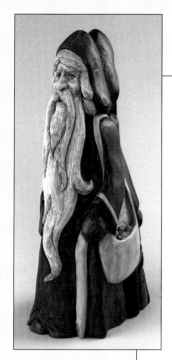

IN THE COLLECTION OF DR. & MRS. MARK KINDRICK

Carole Jean Boyd

John Burke

For many years John Burke has been the source of carving knowledge and technique for hundreds of craftsmen who have read his books or attended his schools and workshops all over the United States. He easily qualifies as the intellectual grandfather of the majority of young carvers working today.

John started woodcarving in the late 1970s by whittling small figures of cowboys and hillbillies. After a few years he went to a Doane College workshop put on by the Omaha Woodcarvers Club. It was here that he discovered mallet-style tools and what they could do. After attending a woodcarving show in Kansas City he realized he needed help. He got that help by taking clay sculpture classes where he learned anatomy. This made a complete turnaround in his work. Gradually John began teaching a few classes, passing along what he had learned and developed.

After 15 years of teaching workshops John retired. He is in the process of starting the investigative process of art to see which way it will take him. John has carved every conceivable kind of wood; but for challenge and spontaneity, he recommends found wood.

The Excitement of Found Wood

John Burke

I've always said that things don't just happen by accident. The best carvings are those that are planned out and have a definite roadmap to follow. I've never been one to carve intense excitement; I prefer to do a soft and dignified thing—a comfortable carving, something you can live with a long time. But found wood makes me change that approach.

Some of my better pieces capture an excitement and vigor unlike much of my other work, and that's mainly because of the nature of the found wood I used. The shapes of found wood are exciting in themselves, so if you have an exciting shape, whatever you carve is going to capture some of that excitement.

There's a learning process with found wood. At first we tend to pick through the collection pile until a piece chooses us. After a while those pieces are gone, and we begin to think of getting another pile. That's when a person's ability to see matures, and he discovers that he can pick up almost any piece of wood and, by using the available lines and planes there, develop something really attractive. I used to do that as a training exercise—just go out and take the first piece of wood off the pile and carve it. I don't mean just do something fast to get it out of the way, but make a strong effort to use the planes that are there to create the shape you have in mind. This exercise taught me a lot of discipline. You have to develop the experience and the only route is just to do it.

I started carving bark because I saw some local carvers working with it. They were using bark from our area, which was all of an inch-and-a-half thick, so little shallow faces were about the only subject they could do. I was absolutely floored when I went into a gallery and saw a carving on a piece of Montana bark five inches wide and five inches thick.

My favorite found woods are juniper and cedar. Their color is wonderful, of course, but their important characteristic is their resistance to disease and rot. When they are downed a lot of woods are infested with worms and bugs and rot away. Dead standing wood is my first choice. It develops a weathered texture that can't be duplicated in water-borne wood. The sapwood gets weathered away and the wood will always retain that white, clean look. This is especially true of western red junipers in Wyoming and western North Dakota. I have carved bristle cone pine and that's a challenge. The pitch and sap, which are always there, make it difficult to work, but the amber color against the dark outside is so spectacular as to make it worth the effort.

When it comes to finishing, I think it's important for people to experiment. I certainly have over the years. In the beginning I tried plain oil finishes, but after a few years they dry out and leave a chalky film. I went through a phase of heavy colorization, too. Now I'm back to monochrome finishes, using either one color of stain or just the natural color of the wood, forgetting about dark accents. On most pieces I seal the surface with a good semi-gloss or matte lacquer and use a dark liquid wax to achieve an antique look. After it dries I buff it hard and put as many coats of clear wax as I want to deepen the shadows.

The best thing about found wood is that it keeps you challenged. You have to shake off old habits and ideas because each piece presents entirely new problems to solve. Trying new things keeps the work fresh and exciting as nothing else can.

John Burke

Carving Found Wood

Debbe Edwards

Wild animal heads on bark are the special provinces of Debbe Edwards' carvings. They sell well, with wolves leading in popularity, followed closely by cougars and bears. Although she has done other subjects, such as Indian heads, she confesses a dedication to forest animals, chiefly because the bark that she favors is an untouched, natural medium perfectly suited to her untamed subjects. Debbe, who lives in Oklahoma, has been carving since 1989.

A professional woodcarver, Debbe teaches classes and workshops throughout the United States and Canada. Combining her love and appreciation of animals with an urge to create, the self-taught artist brings her sculptures to a very lifelike realism. Her attention to detail has been well received at invitational exhibitions throughout the country where she has won awards for her wood and stone sculptures. Some of these exhibitions include the Loveland Sculpture Invitational in Loveland, Colorado; the Danada Sculpture and Art Show in Lombard, Illinois; and the Red Earth Native American Art Show in Oklahoma City, Oklahoma.

Debbe loves the inspiration of each idea, the challenge of creating it, and the respect for it taught to her by her grandfather with whom she spent much of her childhood. Debbe now lives on a farm in Northeast Oklahoma next to her grandfather's farm, still surrounded by animals.

Wild Animals, Wild Bark

Debbe Edwards

Until I saw an Indian head done by Rex Branson I had never seen carving in bark before. I tried a couple of Indian heads but told myself pretty quickly that animals are what I do, so I just started doing them in bark. And kept on doing them. Apparently people like them. The connection between wild animals and wild tree bark seems to be a special relationship. Most people don't have room in their houses now for large pieces of animal sculpture, but I make wall hangings that don't take up a lot of room, so you can have a wolf in your den with no trouble.

Bark presents some special problems to the carver. It's really gritty—deep down gritty—through all the layers. That's hard on your tools, but since there's no cure for it, you just keep sharpening them. Although bark looks tough, it can be fragile, too. The outer layers are thin, and if you try to get down deep too quickly, whole layers can flake off. You have to get down to where the wood is more substantial to do deep carving. That's why every carving is different; you have to obey the wood and pay attention to its structure.

The cleavage problem with bark limits some of the subjects you can consider. For example, horse heads are not very practical. The slender neck would have to protrude from the wood, and the weight of the head could easily snap it off where the thin layers take too much strain. The nose of a wolf sticks out, too, but not so much. Mainly the wild animals I carve have compact heads and stout necks.

Bark has good characteristics, too. There are often surprising little swirls in the wood that you can use in interesting ways. Splits in the wood can be worked into the pattern. I mostly ignore them unless they're going right through an eye. I find that usually I can incorporate the flaws right into the carving.

I don't do much foraging for my own bark. I can't just skim bark off any available log and think it will be suitable for carving. For one thing, the bark has to be dead, and the longer it has been dead the better. Then it has to be thick enough so that I can carve a good-sized animal head that will really stick out. Bark five inches or six inches thick is best. Most of the bark I use I get from North Dakota and Wyoming.

I like to use the entire piece of bark in my carving and sometimes I have to make adjustments from my first idea. Right now I have in reserve a single piece of bark about eight feet long and six inches thick in places. I'm going to have to plan a carving with several animals in it because I refuse to cut it apart. It must have taken three or four hundred years for that piece to grow so thick. Really good bark is getting harder and harder to find.

Power carving is not very useful in my style of carving. I do everything with hand tools. I texture the wood with wood burning tools for the hair and then apply a wash of color and a bit of dry brush. People comment on the lifelike quality of the eyes and often ask if they are inserted glass. They're just paint, but at the end I put a very high gloss on the eyes and nose. I seal the surface of the carving, which brings out the color, and finish with a couple of coats of Minwax, thinned-down with mineral spirits, and a final buffing.

I have carved some other found woods and had an interesting success with juniper, but bark is most appropriate for the wild animal heads I like to do. Each piece of bark presents a unique puzzle for me to solve. A few years ago I carved a fox, a bear and a wolf—all three heads on one piece of bark and each in a different pose. That's the kind of challenge I enjoy.

Debbe Edwards

Debbe Edwards

Debbe Edwards

Gary Falin

Gary has been carving for 30 years and teaching carving for 15 years. For the last three years he has been working as a professional carver and teacher. Prior to carving full time, Gary taught a variety of subjects in secondary school. Today, Gary teaches in carving clubs all over the United States and in several woodcarving schools, such as the J. C. Campbell Folk School and the Tennessee Valley Woodcarving School.

As an award-winning carver, Gary has won first place at the International Woodcarvers Congress and Dollywood Woodcarving Showcase. The Caricature Carvers of America presented him with a special award. He has also been recognized as the feature carver at several shows. In addition to wood carving, Gary is an award-winning pumpkin carver. He was the featured pumpkin carver at Dollywood for five years.

Some of the carvers who have influenced Gary's carving and style include Harold Enlow, Claude Bolton, Eldon Humphries, Pete LeClair, John Burke, Helen Gibson and Phil Bishop.

The Face of Inspiration

Gary Falin

If we had had as many carvers around when I first started carving as we have today, it would have been a lot easier for me to pursue my new found interest. Now there are not only many more carvers but also so many different viewpoints and methods of expression.

Although I still do many different types of carving, I have enjoyed working with the found wood. Presently I'm working on three tree bark pieces: an Indian, a wizard and a traditional Santa. I particularly like caricatures and Santas. My bark pieces usually range between three and five inches thick.

I was first turned on to cottonwood by other carvers. I liked some pieces they had done, and they convinced me how easy it was to work with. It is easy, and it's not just your average piece of wood. It has a lot of irregularities in it, so you can get some inspiration from the form and texture.

I found that using the largest tools possible works really well for me because they get rid of waste wood so much faster. Then I switch to smaller tools and knives for the detail work. And in bark carving I've found you must be very careful with this detail work because small pieces can chip off very easily. You can only carve an eye so many times in the same piece.

I use various forms of sandpaper on some my carvings, but not on bark carvings because it softens up the bark and develops sharp places that need touching up. Scotch Brite is a better substitute on bark. Then I go back and put in some final touches with a V-tool and a knife.

I try to get a particular look out of different pieces of bark. A lot of pieces I finish with paint, and since what I'm looking for is more or less a stain, I use a watered down acrylic. Sometimes it's necessary to alter the paint because the bark is so dark. Over this I use a couple coats of semi-gloss Deft

My inspiration comes from a desire to see finished things and to try out ideas that I find attractive in other peoples' work. I feel like I should pass on the things that I know to others. I have leaned a lot from teaching other's the technique I use. There is nothing more fun than seeing one of your students win a ribbon in a whittling contest. As a matter of fact some of my students have beaten me in whittling contests and carving competitions.

In all my classes, these are the things I tell my students:
- Sharp tools
- Carve on something every day
- Read carving books
- Take seminars
- Don't be afraid to make mistakes
- Ask other people to critique your work
- Practice, practice, practice

Don't be afraid to experiment with your carving. You may be surprised at your results!

Gary Falin

Carving Found Wood

28

Gary Falin

Rick Jensen

Rick Jensen lives in the far northwest corner of Minnesota in Crookston. His signature storybook houses, carved in bark, look like cozy refuges from the cold for tiny woodland sprites. Since 1965, when Rick carved his first whimsical animal for a high school art project, fantasy has always played a major role in his work. He says that he didn't get serious about carving until the early eighties, confessing that the discovery of girls at the same time as carving diverted his attention for a few years.

Rick has won many awards including a People's Choice award and a Judge's Choice Award. He currently teaches his style of bark carving in the upper mid-west.

Unique in Subject & Approach

Rick Jensen

What started me on little houses was a piece of bark that was totally unsuitable for a face-carving. That seemed to be the main thing people did with bark then. I'd met a man in Tacoma, Washington, who put buildings on bark, and I thought this piece might work well for houses. Only I just don't have it in me to do realistic buildings. I make them up depending on the individual piece of bark I have.

It is a kind of signature of mine that I carve the entire piece of bark, leaving only as much of the rough exterior as enhances the carving. The rest might become two, three, four little houses of different sizes, facing different directions. Because the size and shape of the bark piece determines the final carving, I can't duplicate any of my work. I'm pleased to have bark that most carvers reject, the kind with twists and turns and worm holes and rotten places, all of which can contribute to the myth-like quality of the houses.

A steep curve in the surface is another thing I can use. I carve all the way through the piece where I put windows and doors so the houses appear lit from inside. I never plane off the back. In fact I carve the back out and leave the edges so the piece hangs on a wall, not flat but with a lot of space and light behind. That gives the carving life and mystery.

Face-carvers study people's faces and expressions for inspiration. Buildings are my inspiration. When I take a walk I'm looking for unusual windows, rooflines and trims. Old churches are a good source of unique building details. Magazine pictures, even window ads, turn up some good ideas. Half-tumbled-down, rotten buildings in the country give me some good features. It beats going to the mall every day to study faces. I'm not trying to duplicate the buildings I see. I want crooked lines and un-square windows; they add to the charm. What person hasn't got a memory of a really neat tree house he wanted as a kid? I suppose it's the kid in me satisfying that dream with weird houses carved from part of a tree.

I can find some of the bark I use in the river bottoms near my home. Other supplies I buy. I can make better use of thin bark than face carvers can because I hollow out the back then I pierce the piece for windows and doors.

Bark presents some special problems for the carver. Dull tools for one thing. All bark is gritty no matter how hard you work to wash it out. The bark we get around here may have been exposed to flood waters that left a lot of soil, and bark from the prairies has accumulated years of wind-blown grit. And there are pests to contend with: insects, larvae and spiders. I usually seal the bark in a bag and fumigate it.

My favorite finish is Deft semi-gloss. I first spray a couple of coats on the back to seal it, then two or so coats on the front. I rub it down with a brown paper bag and dust it with an air compressor. I build up coats of Deft until I have a slight sheen, and then I rub it down again. I next spray on a coat of matte finish Krylon to take away the sheen, and finally apply a 50-50 mix of Watco light or neutral wax, wipe it off, and buff it off when it dries. I experiment with other finishes, but I like the soft, touch-me finish I get with these materials.

The kind of carving I do depends on what the wood tells me to do. The bark I carve has a lot of history behind it, and I think about the people who have passed by these trees on their way West or the traders who worked along the river banks. There's spirit in the bark that survived all the elements over the years, and I like to think about these events in the past when I'm working.

Rick Jensen

Carving Found Wood

Rick Jensen

Rick Jensen

Carving Found Wood Step-by-Step

Tools

The following is a list of tools and materials used in the step by step carving. Although there are details about which tools and finishes were used in the step by step, it is not essential to use the exact size and sweep. You should use tools you are comfortable with to accomplish the same cuts made in the step by step. The size of the tool will of course depend on the size of the carving:

#5, 50mm (used for rough in work)

#5, 14mm (to separate large masses and create smooth transitional cuts, used for stop cuts)

#5, 8mm (separate smaller masses, help create form and shadows, stop cuts in small areas such as the eyes)

#7, 25mm (develop curvature, smooth clean up)

#7, 18mm (texture, break up surfaces, create soft base structure)

#7, 8mm (create small rounded surfaces, form features such as nose wings, etc.)

#9, 8mm (good transitional tool for small features, e.g. lip to chin structure)

#11, 18mm (used for separating large masses, deep texture, create smooth transitions, e.g. from face to bridge of nose)

#11, 12mm (texturing and separating medium size masses, smooth transition cuts)

#11, 6mm (outline features)

#11, 3mm (create shadows with smooth transition, outline smaller features)

#11, 2mm (small pockets and shadows with smooth lines, good for preparation of wrinkles)

#12, 3mm V-tool (outline small features, create lines and small form, tight shadows)

Detail Knife (several knives were used with this project; however, only one was necessary)

Foredom with mandrel (for Scotch-Brite cleaning)

7440 Scotch-Brite (scuff pad for cleaning)

Small burning tool (used to create soft wrinkles)

Stiff Bristle Brush (cleaning fuzzy and knits from carving)

Deft Semi-Gloss (clear finish material)

Brown paper bag (to burnish the finish)

Wax (finish)

Tooth brush (to apply deep into crevasses)

Soft shoe brush (to buff wax)

1 For this project, a piece of cottonwood bark will be used, which is approximately 42 inches long, 5 inches thick, and 6 inches wide at its widest point. This bark came from a very large dead tree in North Dakota.

2 For the best presentation of a human face in the bark, the carving should be situated in the center. It is not as important to be concerned with the relative amount of carving area as it is the balance of the uncarved portion of the bark. In other words, the top and bottom of the carving should have roughly the same amount of uncarved textured surface. This will add to the over all balance of the presentation.

3 After the balance has been established, the carving area is being evaluated for the most appropriate direction for up and down. To make that selection requires a decision on what will be carved, and how it will fit within the turns, curves, and splits in the bark. It is also important to choose a topic which fits the medium or is sympathetic with the overall presentation or texture. I have chosen to carve a mountain man because of the rough textures, which will surround the piece and the overall feel of outdoors. Another compelling idea is that the size of the bark reminds one of a primal forest. This is the type of environment early mountain men encountered on a daily basis. Therefore, the combination of size and texture relate well to the subject matter selected.

4 Using a #5, 50mm gouge, the bark is removed from the center high point in the carving. A piece of this size could be mounted in various types of holders. For speed and ability to manipulate the piece, it was carved without a holding device. Unless you have a considerable amount of experience, this approach is not recommended.

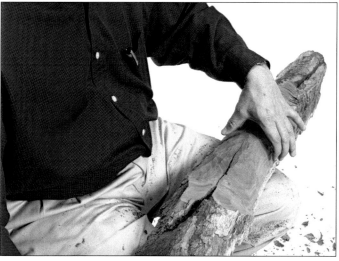

5 One of the problems encountered in carving bark is the presence of cleavage planes or grain separation near the top surface. The deeper you carve into the bark the more solid and fewer cleavage splits. Here the top surface is being removed to reach the solid material.

6 The widest portion of the bark will be used for the center of the face. This will give more room to add accoutrements such as feathers, hair, animal skins, etc., more effectively. Note the u-shaped form of the rough-in. This will allow taper from the center of the face laterally to the sides creating a parabolic arch.

7 This shows the development of the facial "mound". The top and bottom taper away from what will be the tip of the nose.

8 The basic form of the carving is established by creating this tapered mound. Note the pitch of the forehead is severe to create a good profile. Also notice how deep the rough-in goes into the bark. The more depth you can create the more prominent the facial features can be developed. The entire rough-in was developed using the same #5, 50mm gouge.

9 After the mound and tapers are established the outline of the face is drawn. The most important part of the drawing is the center line. This will allow you to develop symmetry in the face more accurately. Asymmetrical faces appear warped and unappealing.

When laying out it is important to follow basic rules of face proportion:

The eyes are in the center of the head. Since this not a three dimensional carving the top of the head will have to be suggested by the pitch and curvature of the hat into a vanishing point. The face is divided into three equal segments from the chin to the bottom of the nose, the bottom of the nose to the brow, and the brow to the hair line.

The face width is half the height of the head or the distance from the chin to the center of the eyes is the width of the face.

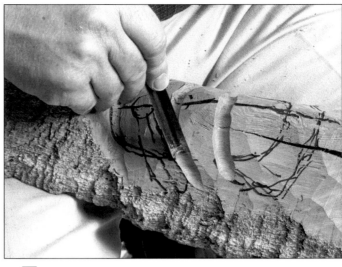

10 The carving begins with the establishment of the bottom of the nose and the brow line. Since this carving has a beard the chin line is not cut nor is the hairline. With these two cuts we dictate the size of the face. A #11, 12mm gouge is used to establish these lines. A wide soft line allows adjustments later on in the project. One pitfall which needs to be avoided is making the face too large for the material. Care should be taken to assure there is plenty of room for hair, animal skins, and feathers.

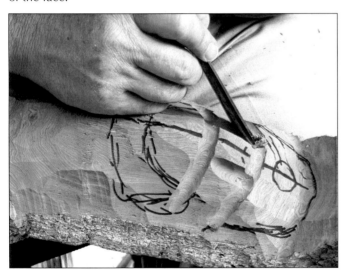

11 Once the nose and brow line are set, the base of the nose is established using the same #11, 12mm gouge. This is cut by running a line parallel to the center line from the horizontal nose cut to the brow line. Note how soft the transition from the cheek to the nose is developing. A typical error here is to taper the nose cut toward the center line at the top. This cut must remain parallel to the center line from the bottom to the top.

12 A #7, 25mm gouge is used to remove the cheek until it is behind the nose. Care is taken to maintain a smooth transition from the nose to the cheek. Here the edge of an old table is used to support the work.

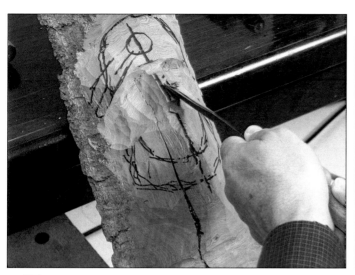

13 Using the same #7, 25mm gouge, the sides of the nose are removed making sure of a soft transition off the face. Care should be taken here to make sure the transition off the nose to the face is at the same angle on both sides of the center line and complete at the same depth on the face.

14 To create enough depth for the hat, the top, upper portion of the nose is taken deeper. This will allow more room for the creation of a cap bill. The lower tip of the nose should not be touched since it is the most forward feature on the face.

15 This profile shows the depth required for a shallow bill on the skin cap. Also note how the surface is smooth from the bridge of the nose across the face.

16 Prior to creating the cap, the hat area is rounded again to prevent the carving from becoming too flat.

17 | Using a #11, 6mm gouge, the bill of the cap is roughed-in. Again a soft tool is used to allow for adjustments in the final location of the bill.

18 | After the bill of the hat is laid in, the tops of the eyelids are drawn for reference and the centerline is redrawn. Here the bottom of the nose is cut in, developing a v-cut toward the center of the nose. This cut is made using a #5, 14mm. This will create a form to install the nares of the nose.

19 | The ball or tip, of the nose is developed using a #7, 8mm gouge. The object here is to make the tip of the nose well rounded.

20 | Starting at the tip of the nose, the #7, 8mm gouge cuts along the edge of the nose at an oblique angle to the face. The wider angles allow for easier adjustment. The base or end of the cut should be into the face. This will create the naris.

21 Using a #7, 8mm gouge, the nose is narrowed above the nares to make the nares the widest part of the nose.

22 The side of the nose is narrowed upward to develop some texture and movement in the lines of the nose and also form the location of the intersection of the cartilage to the bone. This is a slightly wider part of the nose. Keep in mind the inside corner of the eye is in a direct line upward from the edge of the nares.

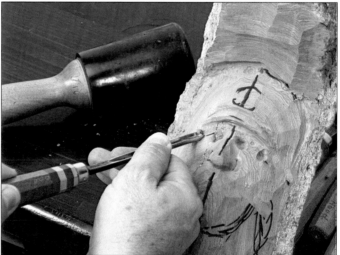

23 This is the completed rough-in for the nose. Detail will be added and refinements made once the entire piece is roughed-in.

24 With a #11, 6mm two holes are cut into the eye area, one against the edge of the nose, the other at the approximate edge of the face. The hole on the outer edge should be deeper to create the eye curvature and allow for peripheral vision.

25 Using the same #11, 6mm gouge, the eyeball is developed by going from the center between the holes and rounding down into the holes.

26 Using a #5, 8mm, the bottom edge of the eye socket is defined and the eyeball better isolated.

27 The eyes are drawn in very narrow in keeping with individuals who spend a lot of time outdoors. The eyes are almost squinted to protect them from the sun and glare, from sand and snow. The top of the eye lid is drawn in and a center line for the eye is drawn perpendicular to the center line down the nose. The horizontal center line helps keep the eyes on the same plane and helps with developing symmetry.

28 Using a #5, 8mm gouge, the sweep is turned down toward the bottom of the face to create this stop cut. I am using a palm tool for this cut; however, it is not necessary. Any #5, 8mm will do the job. The gouge is pressed into the bark with a slight upward angle to help create a shadow line. This cut is the first step to creating the upper eyelid.

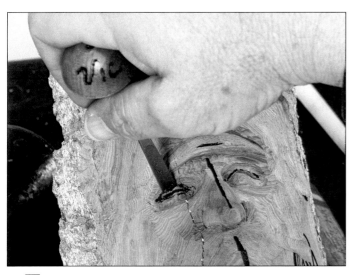

29 The same gouge is pressed into the bark along the line drawn for the upper lid. Again the sweep or curvature is facing downward.

30 The last cut on the upper eyelid is completed in the same manner as the first two cuts, except the sweep is turned up for the last stop cut incision. This gives the upper lid a natural flow. This cut could be completed using a knife; however, using this method assures both eyelids are the same length and shape. Note the finished cut on the opposite side of the face.

31 Using the same #5, 8mm gouge, cut away the lower portion of the eye to the three stop cuts. Be careful to maintain the roundness in the eye which was developed earlier. One good way to assure maintaining the curvature is to make the eyelid a consistent thickness.

32 To create the lower lid cut in a stop cut across the bottom of the eye using the same #5, 8mm gouge. The first cut made on the interior side of the eye is completed with the sweep down. This will create a natural tear duct form.

33 The second stop cut is made on the outside corner. This cut starts just shy of the upper eyelid cut with the sweep facing upward.

34 A knife is used to join the two stop cuts in the middle.

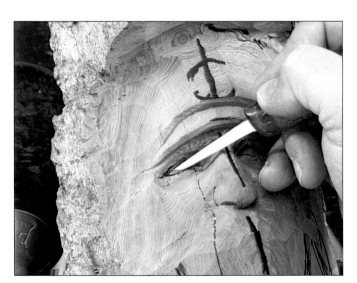

35 Shave the eyeball downward to the lower eyelid. Be very careful to maintain the curvature of the eye. Because the eye sits in the face at a tilt, be sure to cut the lower part of the eyelid deeper to create the proper slant.

36 With the stop cuts completed, the eyeball is roughed-in and the exterior is ready for development.

37 To develop the area below the eye a #11, 6mm gouge is used to channel out for the bags. By removing a semi-circular channel below the eye it will create mass for the development of the bags. This cut should be relatively deep to provide enough material to work with when texturing the eye bags. The left eye shows this cut completed.

38 By using a smaller #11, 3mm, the bag of the eye is better defined. To create an older look, the smaller gouge is run almost vertical on the outside edge. This will result in an eye bag that sags more to the outside and not a perfect curvature. This will aid in developing an older face.

39 To push back the lower lid, create texture in the eye bag, and accentuate the roundness of the eye from top to bottom, a #11, 3mm cut is made under the length of the eyelid.

40 A knife is used to define the corners and the edge of the eye bag. Note the nice deep shadow created by the knife cut and on the right side of the eye.

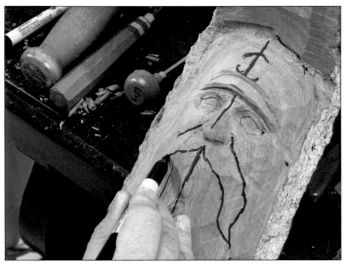

41 The center line is used to lay out the mustache. The mustache does not and should not be perfectly symmetrical; however, the centerline is essential in designing the flow of the hair. Mistakes are often made in laying out the mustache by making them too low, thus forcing the lower lip down toward the chin. When laying out the mustache remember the mouth is approximately two-thirds the distance from the chin to the nose. Therefore the top of the lip is relatively close to the nose.

42 Using a #11, 6mm gouge, the mustache is outlined. Note the top of the mustache is cut in below the nose.

43 The lower edge of the mustache is defined using a #5, 14mm gouge. A #5 sweep is used here to assure flow and curvature. It is important to cut deep here to bring out the mustache. A lot of material is needed for effective development of the mustache hair.

44 To begin laying in the lower lip, a soft tool is used to make sure there is a smooth transition from the chin to the lower lip (#9, 8mm).

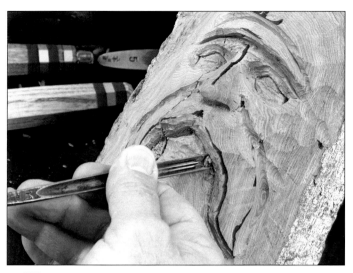

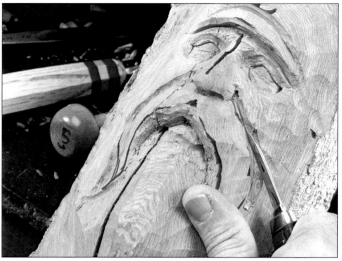

45 A #11, 6mm is used to push the edge of the mouth under the mustache. One of the most common errors here is not developing a steep enough arch in the mouth. One must keep in mind the dental arch is in the shape of a horseshoe. Since the complete mouth is not carved, a vanishing point must be developed which provides the impression the mouth continues on around the face. A deep shadow here does the job.

46 To better define the top of the mustache and develop the laugh line out of the nose, a knife is used to create a deep narrow shadow. This cut is made in the middle of the #11 cut used to separate the cheek from the mustache.

47 A #5, 14mm is used to push the mustache back into the face. In developing this portion of the face it is important to constantly work at keeping the face properly rounded. As features are developed the curvature of the face should be monitored. In addition to rounding the form of the mustache, this cut smooths the hair line into the laugh line.

48 It is important to push the neck in behind the beard. Using a #11, 18mm the neck and shirt lines are laid in place. Depth in this location will also assist in the development of the beard.

49 The front of the face begins to taper inward above the zygomatic arch. The zygomatic arch is the bone that underlies the cheekbone. By going above and below the cheek bone a prominent ridge is formed from the nose around the side of the face. These contours give the face texture and proper form. A by-product of the temple cut is the definition of the visor of the hat.

50 A cut to the temple from the top of the cheek bone will outline the front edge of the face and assist in the development of the cheek bone, as illustrated on the completed right side of the face.

51 To make the cheek bone more prominent a contour cut under the bone will accentuate this feature. This cut has been completed on the right side of the face.

52 To better define the cheekbone, a #7, 18mm gouge is used to create an even contour. The gouge is used with the sweep turned inward to form the bone structure.

53 This profile view illustrates some important points. Notice how prominent the nose is and the angle. The mustache is developed to a point behind the nose. This gives us the proper face contour and prevents the carving from appearing flat. The depth of the neck is critical to pulling out the face. Later the neck depth will be pushed even deeper to create the features of the neck. The profile also reveals the prominence of the cheek bone.

54 Starting with a large #11, 18mm, the beard is given its basic form and texture. It is important to note the flowing nature of the beard and the break up of the outer edge of the hairline. All of the cuts are designed for movement and separation of hair masses. It is also important to note no portion of the beard has the same mass, or surface light value.

55 After the masses are separated and the over all form is established, a smaller #11, 6mm is used to further separate and define hairlines. The edge of the mustache is not left even. The uneven edge to the mustache and the beard add interest and realism to the piece.

56 It is important to show the nasal groove in the hair. This makes the hair part in the center of the face and suggests facial features, which makes the form look natural. A knife was used to under cut the mouth area and define the lower lip.

57 Following the completion of the beard, details of the face are added and refined. Here the brow is being cut in using a #5, 8mm. This cut should be a smooth cut toward the center leaving a rounded edge for the brow.

58 Use a #11, 3mm, to establish the catch-light. Often this technique is used to put a glint or reflection in the eye. Using a knife, cut in the pupil around the iris. Be sure to not make this part of the eye too small. Small, dark pupils will make your piece look angry or mean.

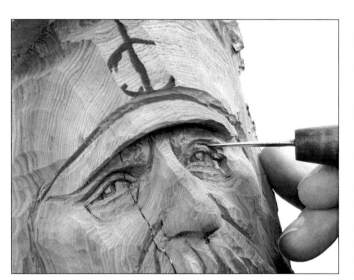

59 The top of the eye lid is cut in using a knife. Be sure to follow the contour of the eyeball. This cut goes at an angle deep into the eye socket creating a deep shadow vanishing point.

60 To create good wrinkles requires starting with a soft tool. Here a #11, 2mm is used to lay in the wrinkles and separate the folds between the wrinkles.

61 A knife cut at the bottom of the wrinkle creates a narrow, definable shadow which makes the wrinkle stand out.

62 The face is mostly completed at this stage. To help develop the image if a mountain man, a collared buck skin shirt with fringe is drawn. The shape of the buck skin shirt is channeled into the crevasse of the bark. This will allow the use of the flaw in the bark to add to our design. An under shirt is also roughed-in to assist in developing shadows and vanishing points. The feather is drawn back onto the hat.

63 The top of the hat is being defined using a #11, 6mm. This tool will help shape the proper angle and prepare for a shadow line.

64 A vanishing point shadow is cut in with a knife. This shadow line will help proportion the carving by providing the illusion that the eyes are in the center of the head. Since we are carving the face only and not the entire head, it is important the proportions be properly suggested.

65 The feather is outlined with a #11, 3mm gouge. It would have been easy to reduce the feather and make it complete. However, in this design it was felt the feather, being broken, would add some interest to the piece.

66 To define the feather edge a knife is used to undercut the perimeter and create a shadow which will separate the feather from the cap.

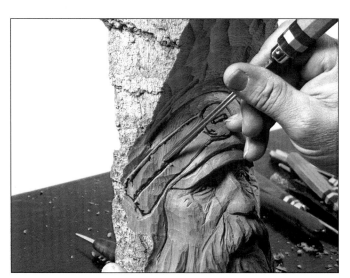

67 The quill of the feather is cut in the same way as the outside edge using a #11, 3mm.

68 To create texture, a #11, 12mm is used to break up the flat surface. By developing an uneven base for the barbs of the feather, the form will not have a rigid, stilted appearance.

69 Following the #11, 12mm pass, a smaller #11, 6mm is used to further break up the surface and begin to develop the lazy "s" form the feather barbs will take.

70 A #12, 3mm V gouge is used to apply the final texture to the feather and create individual barbs.

71 A knife is used to break up the continuous edge of the feather.

72 The quill is rounded using a #5, 8mm. Also the taper of the quill is refined.

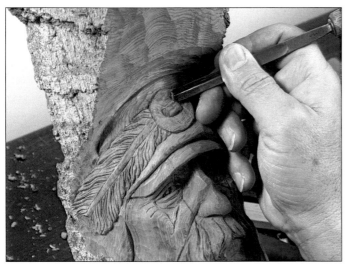

73 The gorget used for the feather attachment is concave and a leather tie is defined.

74 Since there was hair texture on the face and fine line texture on the feather, it was decided to use a completely different style of texture to create the hat. A matted wool or wired hair texture would give the best contrast. To create this texture the surface was broken up using a #11, 12mm gouge. This texture is applied over the entire surface.

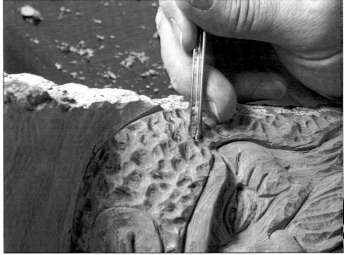

75 A second pass over the surface is done using a #11, 6mm gouge. Care should be taken to leave no flat surfaces for light to reflect off.

76 A third veneer, a #11, 3mm, was used to refine and deepen the texture. Care should be taken to address all of the hat edges.

77 This view shows the start of textured wrinkles on the cheek bone. These were cut in using a #11, 2mm.

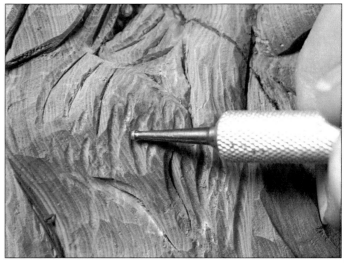

78 A small burnishing tool is used on the face to create subtle wrinkles in the face. This technique compresses the wood fibers to impart a wrinkled texture to the skin. The burnisher is rubbed into the veneer lines and between to create soft wrinkles.

79 The burnish marks add a great deal to the look and feel of this carving. A stiff bristle brush is used to remove all of the loose wood fibers. The entire carving is vigorously brushed, particularly in the tight crevasses.

80 This profile view shows all of the finish cuts used to create emphasis in the carving. The nose line has been changed to emphasize the ball of the nose and to give the nose more interest. This also shows the good contrast achieved in the hat. Notice how uncarved bark is left along the back edge. This will help give the final piece a touch of texture that will contrast nicely with the carving.

81 The collar is outlined and cut using the same method and technique used on the feather. To create the fringe, a #11, 18mm was used to break up the surface and provide a texture, which would provide flow and movement. Flat texture in this situation would make the presentation stiff and stilted. Note how the asymmetrical design of the buckskin shirt is worked into the crack in the bark.

82 Using a small #12, 3mm gouge, the fringe is detailed. Notice that neither the top nor the bottoms of the fringes are at the same level. This will help provide flow and eliminates stiffness.

83 Another technique to add to the fluidity of the presentation is to make sure the fringe is not only uneven, but is lying at various angles. These angles do not need to be severe, a slight turn will add tremendously to the look of the piece. Here a #5, 8mm is being used to under cut one fringe under another.

84 To make the collar appear to go around the neck, a deep shadow is cut into the neck area.

85 This is the completed collar and fringe. To give the collar more lift a deep shadow was cut underneath. The fringe is not stiff or stilted due to the various levels and undulating texture. The collar has an "around the neck" appearance due to proper shadow placement.

86 This is the completed carving prior to clean up and finish. A few more shadow lines were added to the beard and a shadow line was added to the side of the face to separate the face from the hat.

87 Before putting a finish on the carving, Scotch-Brite 7440 is used to clean up the carving. The stiff bristle brush used earlier cleaned the deep cuts, the Scotch-Brite will remove the loose dirt and particles that handling a piece while carving will deposit. Scotch-Brite used on a mandrel will also help soften the harsh edges and help round features, such as wrinkles, feathers, and string. Be sure to wear a dust mask and eye protection while scuffing.

88 The carving is taken outside to apply the finish because of the potential for fumes in the studio. Five coats of clear semi-gloss deft are applied in a quick waving motion.

89 After applying three coats of semi-gloss deft, a wadded paper bag is used to rub down the carving. The last two coats are then applied; a paper bag is rubbed between coats.

90 A wax finish is applied to the carving using a toothbrush. The toothbrush can put wax into the small crevasses and shadow lines. The wax used here is a pure bee's wax with turpentine added for penetration.

91 After the wax dries, a soft, shoe brush is used to buff the carving. Rather than a rag, a brush will get into the entire surface. Buffing the wax will give the carving a deep, rich appearance.

92 By using a #5, 10mm, an undercut arc is made on the back of the bark. This has proven to be the best method for hanging since it does not rely on nails, glue or hangers. It will not come loose and allows the carving to hang plumb.

93 Here is the side profile of the final carving. Note the depth of the carving that allowed a more full development of the facial features.

94 Here is the carving after having been sprayed and buffed with a paper bag.

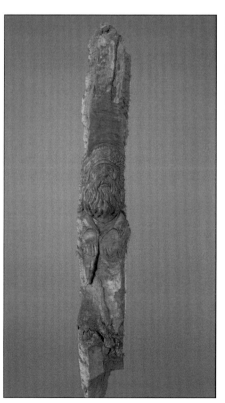

95 By placing the carving in the center of the bark, it gives the carving a sense of balance and symmetry.

96 This is a close up photograph of the finished carving. The applied finish not only provides protection from humidity, thus preventing cracking or checking, but also allows you to keep the carving clean. The finish also helps to accentuate the shadows and highlights creating a more interesting presentation.

I hope you can see from this demonstration some of the possibilities of bark carving.

Reneé Manning

Although Reneé has been working in wood for only four years, she has become an accomplished award-winning carver. She has won Best of Caricature, Best of Spirit and Best of Show. The award she is most proud of is winning first place over more experienced carvers in the whittling and pumpkin carving competition at Dollywood Woodcarving Showcase. Reneé works as an illustrator for the Oak Ridge National Laboratory in Oak Ridge, Tennessee. She is a member of the Foothills Craft Guild and the Tennessee Carvers Guild. Reneé also does clay sculptures and pyrography.

Art From Discarded Wood

Reneé Manning

Before I started carving, I had been exposed to a lot of different carvers while attending classes and shows with my Dad, Ken Manning. I saw carvings that I liked and couldn't afford, but it looked interesting and challenging and something I might enjoy doing, so I tried carving them on my own. I felt like I had arrived when carvers I admire wanted to trade carvings with me.

I specialize in faces, both caricature and realistic, in many kinds of wood. I like working with slab wood because your choices are wide open. Slab wood refers to the pieces of wood that are discarded after the tree has been through the lumbering process. It's more versatile than woods that often dictate your subject and approach. Before I start I sketch out what I want, usually based not just on my own vision but also on pictures I've seen.

I don't know of any places where I can go out and look for wood, so I usually get it at shows or through connections. Right now I'm well stocked, though I am always on the lookout for good pieces.

In carving slabs, I don't use a lot of power tools. Mainly I just use gouges and knives. I typically use a bench knife to remove wood quickly. I have several gouges that I use frequently: a number 5 palm gouge that I use when I am roughing out, a 9 gouge that I use to develop the hair, and a v-tool that I use less

often. I like to go back afterward with a knife to create more of a shadow effect.

For wrinkles around the eyes and on the face, I like to use burnishing tools. I use an angular tool, such as a dental pick to go deeply into the corners of the eyes. I prefer a deep shadow look. To do hair, I use a wide gouge to break up the planes, then a smaller gouge for the smaller planes. I progress to a wide v-tool, a smaller v-tool, and a knife to complete the carving. To create distinction between face and hair, I may add oil paint—often burnt sienna or black and always very translucent—to the boiled linseed oil on one or the other.

I don't use any type of sandpaper or scuffing tools for my pieces. Typically all I use is a dental brush to keep the carving clean throughout the project. I use only a light pencil to draw the lines on a piece and never ink because it soaks into the wood.

I have used acrylics to finish the wood, but I mostly choose linseed oil in combination with oil paints. First, I like to give the carving a base coat of just linseed oil, especially if there is an area that I don't want to color. It is difficult to determine the effect the linseed oil will have, so I like to put it on first. Next I will add a small amount of color to the linseed oil to shade hair or face. Then I spray on four layers of a Krylon satin finish. I also antique it with a Watco satin wax dark color like walnut to emphasize all the deep shadows, making them look even deeper and accenting the detail.

I am inspired by other peoples' work. I try to figure out what I like about a piece and incorporate those characteristics into my own style.

Reneé Manning

Carving Found Wood

Reneé Manning

David Neener

In a sense, the place where he lives dictates David Neener's choice of driftwood as his favorite found wood for carving. His home is in St. Petersburg, Florida, in the middle of the Gulf Coast region where shells and wood wash up on shore in huge quantities. David has found that foraging personally is time-consuming and not very productive, but at least the location gives him sources for purchase of driftwood.

In the thirty years that David has been carving he has won numerous awards for artistic excellence, including the Global Challenge World Championship in Aquatics, People's Choice Award at the Dollywood Woodcarving Showcase and the prestigious People's Choice Award in the Florida Wildlife Exposition. With his marine-inspired wildlife carvings, he is more likely to be seen at art shows rather than at craft gatherings.

David's love of the outdoors and nature is reflected in his love of wood and the creations he develops in wood. As a professional artist, David is thankful to God for his talent and the wonderful medium of driftwood. The collaboration of David's talent and nature's inspiration has led him to title his work "Mother Nature Creations."

Nature's Images, Nature's Wood

David Neener

My first hobby craft class in high school is where I caught my love for working with wood. I still have a funny little dog I did early in my career—a sheltie with peg legs, flat tail and pointy nose. I'm glad I still have it to remind myself that I've come a long way, but it is even more important as a model to young people that I love to teach, just to show that a lot of time and patience and practice can get results.

It was bass fishing that got me into carving marine wildlife, and found wood is ideal for my kind of work. It already has inspiration in it. God blessed me with a particular talent to look at chunks of wood and see things other people do not see. It is a natural product, delivered to your hands just the way Mother Nature made it. This is the most ornate kind of wood you can find to carve. I may pick out a truckload of driftwood at a time, buying it from collectors, and I'm eager to get it home and start discovering the surprises it holds. I can pick up a piece and identify an attractive curve that might become an otter, and the reverse might easily become an eagle.

I especially prize roots with their twists and turns and grain changes. Endless variety presents itself in the tighter grain of the center and looser grain in the limbs of the root system. The look of the piece initially is part of the vision I have for the carving.

Most of the wood I use is decaying, but I get it before the process is complete. Sometimes when the wood is fragile, I compensate for deficiencies by adding fiberglass or resin to build up the structure.

The purists who think only hand tools should be used won't agree with my methods. Let's put it this way: If I could, I would use dynamite. I use a huge assortment of power tools. For roughing in I use a chainsaw or my 20-inch bandsaw with a five-horsepower motor to move a lot of wood quickly. I like to blast directly into the wood and get down to the serious carving.

Because I work on big pieces, sometimes I have to add wood to complete a project. For example, I carve a lot of flying blue herons, starting with a root system. The wings and part of the body are there, but the jutting-out parts—the head and the breast—have to be attached. I use premium grade basswood, plane the attachment side and the driftwood where they will meet, and screw or glue the pieces together. Wood filler will completely hide the joint. Because this will be a painted piece, there's no problem getting a perfect flow from one kind of wood to the other. Grey primer sprayed on the entire carving makes it all look pretty much like driftwood. Then I use acrylics and a lot of different brushes to complete the impression.

In addition to painting, I also finish pieces with clear coating. Depending upon how much of a distressed look I want, I finish only about half. Most I finish completely. I sand the piece with a high-speed rotary flat sander with 80-grit sandpaper. Then I go to 220-grit sandpaper and end by sanding the entire piece by hand. I blow the dust off a couple of times and use a tack rag. When I've regained a dust free environment, I spray on my initial coat of lacquer-based sanding-sealer. After letting it dry for half an hour, I spray on two more coats. I like to use a soft satin finish except in a few instances where high-gloss can achieve a wet look, as with dolphins and turtles.

Sometimes I use sandblasting where a carving can be enhanced with the contrast of a soft, mellow tone against the high finish and color of cedar. After the carving is completed, I mask entirely the area that will receive the clear-coat finish and then sandblast the rest. Then I mask the sandblasted area and apply the final finish by spraying of rubbing it into the previously masked area.

David Neener

David Neener

David Neener

David Neener

Jack Portice

Originally from South Dakota, Jack now lives in Como, Colorado, where he owns Mountain Man Gallery. The gallery is a log structure he disassembled, moved and reconstructed in Como, a little ghost town 10,000 feet high in the mountains. Jack got started carving in an unusual way. A friend of his lost a leg in a motorcycle accident so he decided to carve his friend a wooden stump, and has been carving ever since.

Jack started carving in 1980 and five years later started carving professionally. Since that time he has won numerous Best of Shows, People's Choice Awards, Carver's Choice Awards, and Best of Professional Awards. He and Gene Bass wrote a popular carving book *Carving Weathered Wood*. Jack's found wood of choice is the rare bristle cone pine.

New Life for Age-Old Wood

Jack Portice

I started carving found wood when I moved up to South Park, and bristle cone was the local wood. At that particular time I was working with just anything that I could find, whether it be walnut, a root or cedar. But when we opened our gallery, people wanted a local wood when they came in—bristle cone was it.

Bristle cone pine is the oldest living thing known to man. Most of the wood that I have comes from South Park, where it is collected in the summer because it grows very close to the timberline somewhere between 10,000 and 12,000 feet. We go look areas that have had a major forest fire hundreds of years ago during which the trees fell over leaving the roots exposed to the weather for hundreds of years. The altitude, the location, and how hard it was burned all change the wood.

Some bristle cone gets so hard because it has a lot of pitch in it. Consequently, when it is burned in the fire, the pitch crystallizes and sometimes it is just like glass—extremely hard. In the wood that can be carved, the root really wasn't damaged much by fire but sealed up. When you get into the forest where the wood is more protected it might be more disintegrated, it won't be as hard or firm.

As for slow growth, the trees grow at a rate of one inch in diameter every hundred years, so a tree that is 24 inches wide is 1,200 years old. On the timberline a lot of the tree will die, but a very small portion of that tree will remain alive. Bristle cone pines never grow tall, especially where it's windy. If the trees are protected, they will grow fairly straight.

Bristle cone has been drying for a couple hundred years, consequently no drying process is required. Depending on the piece of wood that you find you can hit pockets of pitch that will actually bubble around the tools and bubble out of the tree. These are little pockets in a root; the whole thing might be fine except for this one area that has a pocket of pitch. I have had pieces where, after I am done, the pitch actually bubbles out of them. I try not to get anything that "pitchy," but it happens every once in a while.

Normally I use standard wood carving gouges, knives and mallets, but there are times when I do power carve some of them to rough them out. I carved a dragon last year that was so fragile that I had to power carve it; the pressure of the gouge would have broken the piece.

Power carving doesn't work well in any bristle cone that has pitch in it. Same thing with sandpaper. But use real sharp tools and find just the right texture of the wood and you get a beautiful glossy finish on the wood itself without using any oil finish—or anything else. I like to use Danish Oil to finish bristle cone because you can brush it on and it brings out the natural color of the wood.

I have two ways of developing a sculpture. One is that I get an idea and then look for a piece of wood that the idea will work in. The second way is to just grab a piece of wood and let it take me wherever it goes. Those are the most fun and the most time consuming, but they also sell the best. People seem to enjoy projects where you just let the wood go. It seems like I get too much stiffness when I try to do a specific thing and make the wood do what I want.

I highly suggest using a vice. I have a vice that was creatively made—with some very unusual parts—for me by a friend. When I am carving I use one hand as a power hand and the other hand as a break. I feel that gives me more control. Also, if I try to hold the wood and carve the wood with one hand, it takes a tremendous amount of time to get anything done.

Jack Portice

Carving Found Wood

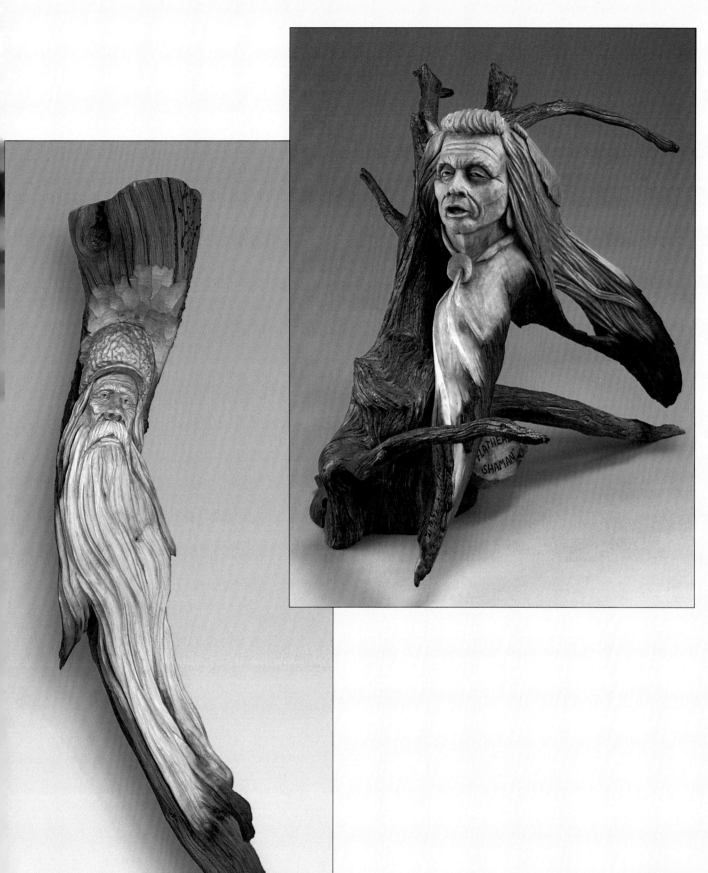

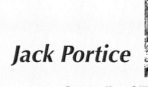

Jack Portice

Jack Portice

Jack Portice

Jim Wright

Jim recently retired from teaching in the Tennessee public school system. He taught eighth grade algebra, and for the last two years he taught fifth grade. He and his wife Carla have two children and one grandson.

Carving since 1986, Jim has acquired many honors. In addition to many blue ribbons and People's Choice Awards, Jim was honored by being selected to carve walking sticks for the Lamar Alexander Presidential Campaign. Mr. Alexander gave these away as favors in his campaign across the United States.

Now a professional carver, Jim's work is currently being collected by many patrons to the point that he primarily does commission work.

Inspiration in Driftwood

Jim Wright

About 14 years ago I started carving. I had been making wooden toys to take to craft fairs and found on the floor some scraps of walnut and cherry that intrigued me. So I carved them and took them along to the next craft fair. My first customer bought a tractor and a wagon and said she'd take a carving, too. The next lady looked at the toys but bought a carving.

What really got me started with found wood was a root from the Black Forest of Germany carved as a face. I had never seen anything like it. I would estimate that by now I have made over a thousand driftwood pieces and an uncounted number of busts and walking sticks.

I do my own foraging for driftwood. I'm lucky to live in an area with a large number of lakes. Fall and winter, and spring before the lakes rise, are the best times. In the summer the lakes are high, and you won't find much.

My all-time favorite driftwood is sassafras. It has a lot of good qualities such as its natural resistance to rot. After its exposure to water, sassafras has a beautiful, natural honey color. Sassafras doesn't have a really strong grain, which helps with fine detail in carving. You can often notice grain going in all directions, so you try to create a carving that fits the particular piece of wood. Sometimes the wood tells you what is going to happen.

I'm also fond of catalpa, osage orange, mulberry and pine. I carve a little hickory and dogwood, too. Sycamore probably has as many interesting shapes as any other driftwood, and of course the lakes around my home are full of cedar.

I do most of my culling while collecting. First, I look for interesting shapes, ones that might suggest faces. Second, I have to determine whether it's big enough for a carving. Then I check to see if it's solid.

Driftwood has to be aged. I usually let it dry for two or three months. Some of it will turn out to be punky when dry. Wood gathered in the winter has less moisture and can be used earlier without checking compared to summer-harvested wood.

I keep a stockpile. When I'm ready to carve I pick out two or three pieces that catch my attention and choose the one I want to work on. Sometimes it is the piece of wood that inspires my ideas. Flowing hair or a beard will pop right out of the wood's grain, maybe suggesting an Indian or a Civil War soldier. But because I carve so many faces I'm always studying the people around me. That's my greatest source of inspiration.

I work entirely with hand tools, almost exclusively with chisel and mallet, though I have two little carving knives that I use for a fine detail on the eyes and wrinkles. I probably do 90 percent of my work with the same eight or ten chisels, regardless of whether I'm working on a face or a walking stick.

When it comes to final finishes, I like to keep it simple. Usually I don't use any finish. I never paint anything because I like to keep the natural color. At most I apply four or five light coats of satin spray. I don't buff between coats and don't use wax or any other topcoat. I try to spray only the carved area so the natural gray color of the driftwood still predominates.

I get a lot of satisfaction out of using only woods I collect in the woods or around the rivers and lakes nearby. For ten years I didn't carve anything else. The only woods I have ever bought are cottonwood bark, cypress knees, and logs, and they constitute a very small part of my work. I can't get excited about working a squared-off piece of wood. A round log that I found myself is a lot more interesting. I find the most inspiration in driftwood.

Jim Wright

Jim Wright

Carving Found Wood

Jim Wright

Jim Wright

About the Authors

Jack Williams

Jack Williams is a retired commercial photographer living in Sun City West, Arizona. He started carving wood in 1973 when he carved an eagle plaque from scrap lumber, not knowing that was not a recommended carving wood. Jack continued to carve birds and competed at the Ward World Wildfowl Competition for ten years. He was first exposed to caricature carving in 1988 at a Harold Enlow class, which had a lasting effect on the direction of his carving. Jack still enjoys carving and studying caricature carving with many great carvers, not only to learn new skills, but to meet interesting people and have a fun time.

His artistic talents have been demonstrated with a third *Best of Show* in the first CCA National Caricature Carving Competition, a *Best of Show* at the Ward Wildfowl Carving Competition, a *Best of Show* at the Dayton Artistry in Wood Show, *People's* and *Carver's Choice* and *Best of Wood Sculpture* at Dollywood, and *Best of Division* at the International Woodcarvers Congress. Jack also won first place in the Flex-Cut Tool Internet Carving Competition in 2001.

October 2005 marked the fourteenth year he coordinated the woodcarving show at Dollywood and the third year to coordinate the National Caricature Carving Competition and Exhibit, also held at Dollywood. Jack became a member of the Caricature Carvers of America in 2003. He is also a founding member of Tennessee Carvers Guild. Jack now spends a great deal of time photographing carvings at shows and for friends. His photography frequently appears in magazines on woodcarving and other subjects.

Along with Vic Hood, Jack co-authored both *Carving Found Wood* and *Extreme Pumpkin Carving*. Jack and Rick Jensen co-authored a book on carving whimsical bark houses titled *Carving Tree Bark*. Most recently, Jack co-authored the book *Carving Cypress Knees* with Carole Jean Boyd. All four books are publishing by Fox Chapel Publishing.

You can e-mail Jack at *carolejack@cox.net*.

Jack Williams & Vic Hood

Vic Hood

Vic Hood is the president of a unique building corporation, Leatherwood, Inc., which specializes in historic restoration. As a restorationist, Vic has been responsible for the restoration of several presidential houses, a few national landmarks, national monuments, and house museums. He started carving in 1991, concentrating on carving full-sized human busts for which he has won 83 awards including several *Best of Show* awards. His most treasured honor was to be selected to create a Christmas ornament for the White House in 2001. Vic is one of the founders of the Leipers Fork Carving Club in Leipers Fork, Tennessee.

Vic studied under John Burke and Larry Rogers for several years before becoming a carving instructor himself. He currently teaches classes in carving the human bust, as well as subjects carved in found wood, at several major workshops around the country and at individual club workshops. Although best known for his bust carving, Vic has created hundreds of carvings in found wood.

Vic is available to teach classes. You may contact him by e-mail at *vhood@leatherwoodinc.com*.

Vic Hood

Vic Hood

Carving Found Wood **87**

Jack Williams

Jack Williams

More Great Books from Fox Chapel Publishing

The Little Book of Whittling
Passing Time on the Trail, on the Porch, and Under the Stars
By Chris Lubkemann

Unwind while you learn to create useful and whimsical objects with nothing more than a pocket knife, a twig, and a few minutes of time.

ISBN: 978-1-56523-274-7
$12.95 • 104 Pages

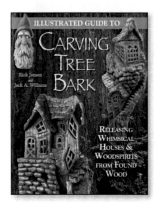

Illustrated Guide to Carving Tree Bark
Releasing Whimsical Houses ar Woodspirits from Found Wood
By Rick Jensen, Jack A. Williams

Carving found wood has never been easier with step-by-step instructions for releasing whimsical bark animals, wood spirits, Santas, and more.

ISBN: 978-1-56523-218-1
$14.95 • 80 Pages

Tree Craft
35 Rustic Projects that Bring the Outdoors In
By Chris Lubkemann

Beautify your home with rustic accents and helpful items made from twigs, branches, logs, and other found wood. Over 35 easy-to-make projects for everything from a coat rack to candle holders.

ISBN: 978-1-56523-455-0
$19.95 • 128 Pages

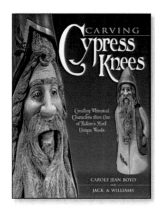

Carving Cypress Knees
Creating Whimsical Characters from One of Nature's Most Unique Woods
By Carole Jean Boyd, Jack A. Williams

Unlock whimsical characters and wood spirits from within one of nature's most unique woods.

ISBN: 978-1-56523-271-6
$17.95 • 96 Pages

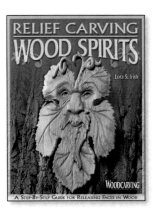

Relief Carving Wood Spirits
A Step-By-Step Guide for Releasing Faces in Wood
By Lora S. Irish

Learn the enjoyable craft of relief carving as you create ten of your very own wood spirits. Every step of relief carving is carefully illustrated and explained, from preparing the wood to evaluating the cuts.

ISBN: 978-1-56523-333-1
$19.95 • 136 Pages

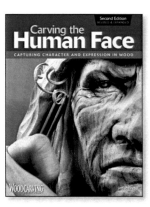

Carving the Human Face 2nd Edition, Revised & Expanded
Capturing Character and Expression in Wood
By Jeff Phares

Follow 350+ color photos and 50 drawi that provide useful anatomical referenc to create realistic portraits in wood from champion carver.

ISBN: 978-1-56523-424-6
$24.95 • 144 Pages

Look for These Books at Your Local Bookstore or Woodworking Retailer
To order direct, call **800-457-9112** or visit *www.FoxChapelPublishing.com*
By mail, please send check or money order + $4.00 per book for S&H to: Fox Chapel Publishing, 903 Square Street, Mount Joy, PA 17552